50 Sandwich for Every Taste Recipes for Home

By: Kelly Johnson

Table of Contents

- Classic BLT (Bacon, Lettuce, Tomato)
- Turkey Avocado Club
- Grilled Cheese with Tomato Soup
- Caprese Sandwich with Basil Pesto
- Pulled Pork Sandwich with Coleslaw
- Roast Beef and Horseradish Mayo
- Vegetarian Hummus and Veggie Wrap
- Egg Salad Sandwich with Dill
- Tuna Salad with Celery and Mayo
- Cuban Sandwich with Pickles and Mustard
- Philly Cheesesteak with Onions and Peppers
- Buffalo Chicken Sandwich with Blue Cheese
- Chicken Caesar Wrap
- Pastrami on Rye with Mustard
- Falafel Wrap with Tzatziki
- Spicy Shrimp Po' Boy
- Avocado Toast with Radishes and Feta
- Meatball Sub with Marinara and Mozzarella
- Smoked Salmon and Cream Cheese Bagel
- BBQ Chicken Sandwich with Pickles
- Greek Pita with Tzatziki and Veggies
- Pimento Cheese Sandwich on White Bread
- Eggplant Parmesan Sandwich
- Roasted Vegetable and Goat Cheese Sandwich
- Banh Mi with Pickled Vegetables
- Cheddar and Chutney Sandwich
- Spinach and Feta Stuffed Pita
- Lobster Roll with Lemon Butter
- Chicken Salad with Grapes and Walnuts
- Smashed Chickpea Salad Sandwich

- Italian Sub with Salami and Provolone
- Pork Schnitzel Sandwich with Cabbage Slaw
- Tandoori Chicken Wrap with Mint Yogurt
- Caprese Panini with Mozzarella and Tomatoes
- Bacon, Egg, and Cheese Breakfast Sandwich
- Vegan Lentil Burger Sandwich
- Crispy Fish Tacos with Cabbage Slaw
- Turkey and Cranberry Sauce Sandwich
- Jerk Chicken Sandwich with Mango Salsa
- Peanut Butter and Banana Sandwich
- Sweet and Spicy Pork Bahn Mi
- Crispy Chicken Sandwich with Pickles
- Muffuletta with Olive Salad
- Roasted Beet and Goat Cheese Sandwich
- Salami and Cheese Sandwich with Mustard
- Mushroom and Swiss Burger
- Tzatziki Chicken Wrap
- Honey Mustard Ham and Cheese Sandwich
- Chickpea and Avocado Smash Sandwich
- Sweet Potato and Black Bean Sandwich

Classic BLT (Bacon, Lettuce, Tomato)

Ingredients:

- 4 slices of bacon
- 2 slices of bread (your choice)
- 1 large tomato, sliced
- Lettuce leaves (romaine or iceberg)
- Mayonnaise
- Salt and pepper to taste

Instructions:

1. Cook the bacon in a skillet over medium heat until crispy. Drain on paper towels.
2. Toast the bread slices until golden brown.
3. Spread mayonnaise on one side of each slice of bread. Layer bacon, tomato slices, and lettuce on one slice. Season with salt and pepper.
4. Top with the second slice of bread, mayo side down. Slice in half and serve immediately.

Turkey Avocado Club

Ingredients:

- 3 slices of bread (white or whole grain)
- 4 ounces sliced turkey breast
- 2 slices of bacon, cooked
- 1/2 avocado, sliced
- Lettuce leaves
- Tomato, sliced
- Mayonnaise
- Salt and pepper to taste

Instructions:

1. Toast the bread slices until golden brown.
2. Spread mayonnaise on one side of each slice of bread.
3. Layer turkey, bacon, avocado, lettuce, and tomato on the first slice. Season with salt and pepper.
4. Place the second slice of bread on top and repeat the layering process. Finish with the last slice of bread on top.
5. Secure with toothpicks if desired, then slice and serve.

Grilled Cheese with Tomato Soup

Ingredients:

- 2 slices of bread (your choice)
- 2 slices of cheese (cheddar, American, or your choice)
- 1 tablespoon butter
- 1 can (about 15 ounces) tomato soup
- Salt and pepper to taste

Instructions:

1. In a saucepan, heat the tomato soup over medium heat, seasoning with salt and pepper. Stir occasionally until hot.
2. Heat a skillet over medium heat. Butter one side of each bread slice.
3. Place one slice, butter side down, in the skillet. Add cheese slices on top, then cover with the second slice of bread, butter side up.
4. Cook until golden brown, about 3-4 minutes on each side, flipping carefully.
5. Serve the grilled cheese alongside the hot tomato soup for dipping.

Caprese Sandwich with Basil Pesto

Ingredients:

- 2 slices of fresh mozzarella cheese
- 1 large tomato, sliced
- Fresh basil leaves
- 2 slices of bread (ciabatta or focaccia)
- 2 tablespoons basil pesto
- Balsamic glaze (optional)

Instructions:

1. Toast the bread slices lightly.
2. Spread basil pesto on one side of each slice of bread.
3. Layer mozzarella slices, tomato slices, and fresh basil leaves on one slice of bread.
4. Drizzle with balsamic glaze if desired, then top with the second slice of bread, pesto side down.
5. Serve immediately or press down slightly and grill for a warm sandwich.

Pulled Pork Sandwich with Coleslaw

Ingredients:

- 1 cup pulled pork (cooked)
- 2 slices of bread or hamburger buns
- 1/2 cup coleslaw
- Barbecue sauce (optional)

Instructions:

1. Warm the pulled pork in a saucepan or microwave.
2. If desired, mix in barbecue sauce to the pulled pork.
3. Place the pulled pork on one slice of bread or the bottom half of a bun.
4. Top with coleslaw and place the other slice of bread or bun on top.
5. Serve immediately.

Roast Beef and Horseradish Mayo

Ingredients:

- 4 ounces thinly sliced roast beef
- 2 slices of bread (your choice)
- 1 tablespoon horseradish sauce
- 1 tablespoon mayonnaise
- Lettuce leaves
- Tomato, sliced
- Salt and pepper to taste

Instructions:

1. In a small bowl, mix together horseradish sauce and mayonnaise.
2. Spread the horseradish mayo on one side of each slice of bread.
3. Layer roast beef, lettuce, and tomato on one slice. Season with salt and pepper.
4. Top with the second slice of bread, mayo side down. Slice in half and serve.

Vegetarian Hummus and Veggie Wrap

Ingredients:

- 1 large tortilla or wrap
- 1/2 cup hummus
- 1/2 cucumber, sliced
- 1 carrot, grated
- 1 bell pepper, sliced
- Handful of spinach or mixed greens
- Feta cheese (optional)
- Olive oil (optional)

Instructions:

1. Spread hummus evenly over the tortilla.
2. Layer cucumber, carrot, bell pepper, spinach, and feta cheese on top.
3. Drizzle with olive oil if desired.
4. Roll the tortilla tightly, tucking in the ends as you go. Slice in half and serve.

Enjoy these delicious sandwiches and wraps!

Egg Salad Sandwich with Dill

Ingredients:

- 4 hard-boiled eggs, chopped
- 2 tablespoons mayonnaise
- 1 teaspoon Dijon mustard
- 1 tablespoon fresh dill, chopped
- Salt and pepper to taste
- 2 slices of bread (your choice)

Instructions:

1. In a bowl, combine chopped eggs, mayonnaise, Dijon mustard, dill, salt, and pepper. Mix until well combined.
2. Spread the egg salad mixture onto one slice of bread. Top with the second slice of bread.
3. Slice in half and serve immediately.

Tuna Salad with Celery and Mayo

Ingredients:

- 1 can (about 5 ounces) tuna, drained
- 2 tablespoons mayonnaise
- 1/4 cup celery, diced
- 1 tablespoon onion, diced (optional)
- Salt and pepper to taste
- 2 slices of bread (your choice)

Instructions:

1. In a bowl, combine drained tuna, mayonnaise, celery, onion (if using), salt, and pepper. Mix well.
2. Spread the tuna salad on one slice of bread. Top with the second slice of bread.
3. Slice in half and serve.

Cuban Sandwich with Pickles and Mustard

Ingredients:

- 2 slices of Cuban bread or hoagie rolls
- 3 ounces sliced roast pork
- 3 ounces sliced ham
- 2 slices Swiss cheese
- Dill pickles, sliced
- Yellow mustard

Instructions:

1. Preheat a panini press or skillet.
2. Spread mustard on the inside of both slices of bread.
3. Layer roast pork, ham, Swiss cheese, and dill pickles on one slice of bread.
4. Top with the other slice of bread, pressing down slightly.
5. Grill in the panini press or skillet until golden brown and the cheese melts.
6. Slice and serve.

Philly Cheesesteak with Onions and Peppers

Ingredients:

- 8 ounces ribeye steak, thinly sliced
- 1 tablespoon olive oil
- 1/2 onion, sliced
- 1/2 bell pepper, sliced
- 2 slices provolone cheese
- 1 hoagie roll

Instructions:

1. In a skillet, heat olive oil over medium heat. Add onions and bell peppers and sauté until soft.
2. Add sliced steak to the skillet and cook until browned, about 3-4 minutes.
3. Place provolone cheese on top of the steak mixture and cover until melted.
4. Spoon the mixture into the hoagie roll and serve.

Buffalo Chicken Sandwich with Blue Cheese

Ingredients:

- 1 chicken breast, cooked and shredded
- 1/4 cup buffalo sauce
- 2 slices of bread or a bun
- 1/4 cup blue cheese crumbles
- Lettuce leaves (optional)

Instructions:

1. In a bowl, mix shredded chicken with buffalo sauce until well coated.
2. Toast the bread or bun lightly.
3. Place the buffalo chicken on one slice of bread or the bottom half of the bun. Top with blue cheese crumbles and lettuce if desired.
4. Add the second slice of bread or bun top and serve.

Chicken Caesar Wrap

Ingredients:

- 1 large tortilla
- 1 cup cooked chicken, diced
- 1/2 cup romaine lettuce, chopped
- 2 tablespoons Caesar dressing
- Grated Parmesan cheese (optional)

Instructions:

1. In a bowl, combine diced chicken, romaine lettuce, Caesar dressing, and Parmesan cheese if using. Mix well.
2. Spread the mixture in the center of the tortilla.
3. Fold in the sides and roll up tightly to form a wrap.
4. Slice in half and serve.

Pastrami on Rye with Mustard

Ingredients:

- 4 ounces sliced pastrami
- 2 slices rye bread
- Yellow mustard
- Pickles (optional)

Instructions:

1. Toast the rye bread lightly if desired.
2. Spread mustard on one side of each slice of bread.
3. Layer pastrami on one slice of bread. Add pickles if desired.
4. Top with the second slice of bread, mustard side down. Slice in half and serve.

Enjoy these delicious sandwiches!

Falafel Wrap with Tzatziki

Ingredients:

- 4-6 falafel balls (store-bought or homemade)
- 1 large tortilla or pita bread
- 1/2 cup lettuce, shredded
- 1/4 cup tomatoes, diced
- 1/4 cup cucumber, diced
- 1/4 cup tzatziki sauce

Instructions:

1. Cook the falafel according to package instructions or until crispy if homemade.
2. In the center of the tortilla or pita, layer the lettuce, tomatoes, cucumbers, and falafel.
3. Drizzle tzatziki sauce over the top.
4. Roll the wrap tightly and slice in half to serve.

Spicy Shrimp Po' Boy

Ingredients:

- 8 ounces shrimp, peeled and deveined
- 1/2 cup buttermilk
- 1/2 cup cornmeal
- 1 teaspoon cayenne pepper
- 1 French baguette
- Lettuce, shredded
- Sliced tomatoes
- Remoulade sauce (or mayonnaise mixed with hot sauce)

Instructions:

1. Preheat the oven to 400°F (200°C). In a bowl, soak the shrimp in buttermilk.
2. In another bowl, mix cornmeal, cayenne pepper, salt, and pepper. Dredge shrimp in the cornmeal mixture.
3. Place shrimp on a baking sheet and bake for 10-12 minutes, until cooked through and crispy.
4. Slice the baguette and spread remoulade sauce on both sides.
5. Layer shrimp, lettuce, and tomatoes in the sandwich and serve.

Avocado Toast with Radishes and Feta

Ingredients:

- 1 slice of whole-grain bread
- 1/2 ripe avocado
- 4-5 radishes, thinly sliced
- 2 tablespoons feta cheese, crumbled
- Olive oil, for drizzling
- Salt and pepper to taste

Instructions:

1. Toast the slice of bread to your liking.
2. Mash the avocado in a bowl and season with salt and pepper.
3. Spread the mashed avocado over the toasted bread.
4. Top with sliced radishes and crumbled feta cheese. Drizzle with olive oil before serving.

Meatball Sub with Marinara and Mozzarella

Ingredients:

- 4-6 meatballs (homemade or store-bought)
- 1 cup marinara sauce
- 1 sub roll or hoagie
- 1/2 cup mozzarella cheese, shredded

Instructions:

1. Preheat the oven to 350°F (175°C). In a saucepan, heat marinara sauce and add meatballs, cooking until warmed through.
2. Place the sub roll on a baking sheet and spoon the meatballs and sauce into the roll.
3. Top with mozzarella cheese and bake for about 10 minutes, or until the cheese is melted and bubbly.
4. Serve hot.

Smoked Salmon and Cream Cheese Bagel

Ingredients:

- 1 bagel, sliced
- 2 tablespoons cream cheese
- 4 ounces smoked salmon
- Capers (optional)
- Sliced red onion (optional)
- Fresh dill (optional)

Instructions:

1. Toast the bagel halves until golden brown.
2. Spread cream cheese generously on each half of the bagel.
3. Layer smoked salmon on top. Add capers, sliced red onion, and fresh dill if desired.
4. Serve immediately.

BBQ Chicken Sandwich with Pickles

Ingredients:

- 1 cup cooked chicken, shredded
- 1/2 cup BBQ sauce
- 1 hamburger bun
- Pickles, for topping

Instructions:

1. In a bowl, mix shredded chicken with BBQ sauce until well coated.
2. Toast the hamburger bun if desired. Spoon BBQ chicken onto the bottom half of the bun.
3. Top with pickles and cover with the top half of the bun. Serve warm.

Greek Pita with Tzatziki and Veggies

Ingredients:

- 1 pita bread
- 1/2 cup tzatziki sauce
- 1/2 cucumber, sliced
- 1/2 bell pepper, sliced
- 1/4 red onion, sliced
- Lettuce, shredded

Instructions:

1. Warm the pita bread slightly in the oven or microwave.
2. Spread tzatziki sauce inside the pita.
3. Fill with cucumber, bell pepper, red onion, and lettuce.
4. Serve immediately as a fresh, light meal.

Enjoy these delicious sandwiches and wraps!

Pimento Cheese Sandwich on White Bread

Ingredients:

- 1 cup pimento cheese spread (store-bought or homemade)
- 2 slices of white bread
- Lettuce leaves (optional)
- Tomato slices (optional)

Instructions:

1. Spread a generous amount of pimento cheese on one slice of bread.
2. Add lettuce and tomato slices if desired.
3. Top with the second slice of bread, cut in half, and serve.

Eggplant Parmesan Sandwich

Ingredients:

- 1 medium eggplant, sliced
- 1 cup marinara sauce
- 1 cup mozzarella cheese, shredded
- 1/2 cup Parmesan cheese, grated
- 1 baguette or Italian roll
- Olive oil, for brushing
- Salt and pepper to taste

Instructions:

1. Preheat the oven to 375°F (190°C). Season eggplant slices with salt and let sit for 30 minutes to draw out moisture. Rinse and pat dry.
2. Brush eggplant with olive oil and bake for 20-25 minutes until tender.
3. Slice the baguette and layer with marinara sauce, baked eggplant, mozzarella, and Parmesan cheese.
4. Bake the sandwich for an additional 10 minutes or until the cheese is melted and bubbly. Serve hot.

Roasted Vegetable and Goat Cheese Sandwich

Ingredients:

- 1 zucchini, sliced
- 1 bell pepper, sliced
- 1 red onion, sliced
- 1 cup cherry tomatoes, halved
- 1 tablespoon olive oil
- Salt and pepper to taste
- 4 ounces goat cheese
- 2 slices of whole-grain or sourdough bread

Instructions:

1. Preheat the oven to 400°F (200°C). Toss zucchini, bell pepper, red onion, and cherry tomatoes with olive oil, salt, and pepper.
2. Spread the vegetables on a baking sheet and roast for 20-25 minutes until tender.
3. Spread goat cheese on one slice of bread, layer roasted vegetables on top, and cover with the other slice. Serve warm.

Banh Mi with Pickled Vegetables

Ingredients:

- 1 baguette
- 1/2 cup pickled carrots and daikon radish (store-bought or homemade)
- 1/2 cucumber, sliced
- 1/2 pound grilled pork, chicken, or tofu
- Fresh cilantro
- Sriracha (optional)

Instructions:

1. Slice the baguette in half and lightly toast it.
2. Layer pickled vegetables, sliced cucumber, and protein of choice inside the baguette.
3. Add fresh cilantro and drizzle with Sriracha if desired. Close the sandwich and serve.

Cheddar and Chutney Sandwich

Ingredients:

- 2 slices of bread (white or whole-grain)
- 2 ounces sharp cheddar cheese, sliced
- 2 tablespoons chutney (mango or onion)

Instructions:

1. Spread chutney on one slice of bread.
2. Top with cheddar cheese and cover with the second slice of bread.
3. Optionally, grill the sandwich in a pan until golden brown and the cheese is melted. Serve warm.

Spinach and Feta Stuffed Pita

Ingredients:

- 1 whole wheat pita
- 1 cup fresh spinach, chopped
- 1/2 cup feta cheese, crumbled
- 1/4 cup Greek yogurt (for dressing)
- Salt and pepper to taste

Instructions:

1. In a bowl, mix spinach, feta cheese, Greek yogurt, salt, and pepper.
2. Cut the pita in half to form pockets.
3. Stuff each half with the spinach and feta mixture. Serve immediately.

Lobster Roll with Lemon Butter

Ingredients:

- 1 pound cooked lobster meat, chopped
- 2 tablespoons butter, melted
- 1 tablespoon lemon juice
- 2 hot dog buns or soft rolls
- Lettuce leaves
- Salt and pepper to taste

Instructions:

1. In a bowl, mix chopped lobster meat with melted butter, lemon juice, salt, and pepper.
2. Toast the hot dog buns lightly if desired.
3. Fill each bun with lettuce leaves and lobster mixture. Serve chilled or at room temperature.

Enjoy these delicious sandwiches!

Chicken Salad with Grapes and Walnuts

Ingredients:

- 2 cups cooked chicken breast, shredded
- 1 cup seedless grapes, halved (red or green)
- 1/2 cup walnuts, chopped
- 1/2 cup mayonnaise
- 1 tablespoon Dijon mustard
- 1 tablespoon lemon juice
- Salt and pepper to taste
- Lettuce leaves (for serving)
- Optional: celery, chopped (for added crunch)

Instructions:

1. In a large bowl, combine shredded chicken, halved grapes, chopped walnuts, and optional celery.
2. In a separate bowl, whisk together mayonnaise, Dijon mustard, lemon juice, salt, and pepper.
3. Pour the dressing over the chicken mixture and toss gently to combine.
4. Serve on a bed of lettuce leaves or in a sandwich.

Smashed Chickpea Salad Sandwich

Ingredients:

- 1 can (15 ounces) chickpeas, drained and rinsed
- 1/4 cup mayonnaise or Greek yogurt
- 1 tablespoon Dijon mustard
- 1 tablespoon lemon juice
- 1/4 cup celery, diced
- 1/4 cup red onion, diced
- Salt and pepper to taste
- 4 slices of whole-grain bread or wraps
- Lettuce leaves (for serving)

Instructions:

1. In a bowl, lightly smash the chickpeas with a fork, leaving some whole for texture.
2. Stir in mayonnaise, Dijon mustard, lemon juice, diced celery, diced red onion, salt, and pepper until well combined.
3. Spoon the chickpea salad onto slices of whole-grain bread or wraps.
4. Top with lettuce leaves, cover with another slice of bread, and serve.

Enjoy these nutritious and tasty salads!

Italian Sub with Salami and Provolone

Ingredients:

- 1 hoagie roll
- 4 ounces salami, sliced
- 4 ounces provolone cheese, sliced
- Lettuce leaves
- Tomato, sliced
- Red onion, thinly sliced
- Italian dressing
- Olive oil and vinegar (optional)
- Salt and pepper to taste

Instructions:

1. Slice the hoagie roll in half and drizzle with olive oil and vinegar if desired.
2. Layer the salami and provolone cheese on the bottom half.
3. Add lettuce, tomato slices, and red onion.
4. Drizzle with Italian dressing and season with salt and pepper.
5. Close the sandwich and cut it in half to serve.

Pork Schnitzel Sandwich with Cabbage Slaw

Ingredients:

- 2 pork cutlets
- Salt and pepper to taste
- 1/2 cup flour
- 1 egg, beaten
- 1 cup breadcrumbs
- Oil for frying
- 1 hamburger bun or crusty bread
- Cabbage slaw (store-bought or homemade)

Instructions:

1. Season the pork cutlets with salt and pepper.
2. Dredge each cutlet in flour, dip in beaten egg, and coat with breadcrumbs.
3. Heat oil in a skillet over medium heat and fry the cutlets until golden brown, about 4-5 minutes per side.
4. Toast the bun and place the schnitzel on it.
5. Top with cabbage slaw and serve.

Tandoori Chicken Wrap with Mint Yogurt

Ingredients:

- 1 cup cooked tandoori chicken, shredded
- 1 large tortilla or wrap
- Lettuce leaves
- 1/2 cucumber, sliced
- 1/4 red onion, thinly sliced
- 1/2 cup plain yogurt
- 1 tablespoon fresh mint, chopped
- Salt and pepper to taste

Instructions:

1. In a small bowl, mix the yogurt with chopped mint, salt, and pepper to create the mint yogurt sauce.
2. Spread the mint yogurt sauce over the tortilla.
3. Layer with lettuce, tandoori chicken, cucumber slices, and red onion.
4. Roll the wrap tightly, slice in half, and serve.

Caprese Panini with Mozzarella and Tomatoes

Ingredients:

- 2 slices of ciabatta or Italian bread
- 4 ounces fresh mozzarella cheese, sliced
- 1 medium tomato, sliced
- Fresh basil leaves
- Olive oil
- Balsamic glaze (optional)
- Salt and pepper to taste

Instructions:

1. Preheat a panini press or skillet over medium heat.
2. Drizzle olive oil on one side of each slice of bread.
3. Layer mozzarella, tomato slices, and basil leaves on the un-oiled sides.
4. Season with salt and pepper, and drizzle with balsamic glaze if desired.
5. Close the sandwich and grill until golden brown and the cheese melts, about 3-4 minutes. Serve warm.

Bacon, Egg, and Cheese Breakfast Sandwich

Ingredients:

- 2 slices of bread or a bagel
- 2 slices of bacon
- 1 egg
- 1 slice of cheese (cheddar or American)
- Salt and pepper to taste
- Butter (for cooking)

Instructions:

1. In a skillet, cook the bacon until crispy. Remove and set aside.
2. In the same skillet, melt a small amount of butter and crack the egg into the pan. Cook to your liking (sunny-side-up or scrambled).
3. Toast the bread or bagel.
4. Assemble the sandwich: layer bacon, cooked egg, and cheese on one slice of bread. Top with the other slice.
5. Serve warm.

Vegan Lentil Burger Sandwich

Ingredients:

- 1 cup cooked lentils
- 1/2 cup breadcrumbs
- 1/4 cup chopped onion
- 1 clove garlic, minced
- 1 tablespoon soy sauce
- Salt and pepper to taste
- Burger buns
- Lettuce, tomato, and avocado for topping

Instructions:

1. In a bowl, mash the cooked lentils with a fork, leaving some whole.
2. Mix in breadcrumbs, onion, garlic, soy sauce, salt, and pepper until combined.
3. Form the mixture into patties.
4. Cook in a skillet over medium heat until browned on both sides.
5. Serve on burger buns with lettuce, tomato, and avocado.

Crispy Fish Tacos with Cabbage Slaw

Ingredients:

- 2 fillets of white fish (such as cod or tilapia)
- 1/2 cup flour
- 1 egg, beaten
- 1 cup cornmeal
- Oil for frying
- Corn tortillas
- Cabbage slaw (store-bought or homemade)
- Lime wedges for serving

Instructions:

1. Season the fish fillets with salt and pepper.
2. Dredge each fillet in flour, dip in beaten egg, and coat with cornmeal.
3. Heat oil in a skillet over medium-high heat and fry the fish until golden brown and cooked through, about 4-5 minutes per side.
4. Warm the corn tortillas in a dry skillet or microwave.
5. Assemble the tacos by placing the crispy fish on the tortillas and topping with cabbage slaw. Serve with lime wedges.

Enjoy these delicious sandwiches and wraps!

Turkey and Cranberry Sauce Sandwich

Ingredients:

- 2 slices of whole grain or sourdough bread
- 4-6 slices of turkey breast
- 2 tablespoons cranberry sauce
- Lettuce leaves
- Slices of Swiss or cheddar cheese (optional)
- Salt and pepper to taste

Instructions:

1. Spread cranberry sauce on one slice of bread.
2. Layer with turkey slices and cheese if using.
3. Add lettuce and season with salt and pepper.
4. Top with the second slice of bread and cut in half to serve.

Jerk Chicken Sandwich with Mango Salsa

Ingredients:

- 1 boneless chicken breast
- 2 tablespoons jerk seasoning
- 1 hamburger bun
- Lettuce or arugula
- 1/2 mango, diced
- 1/4 red onion, finely chopped
- 1 lime, juiced
- Salt to taste

Instructions:

1. Rub the chicken breast with jerk seasoning and grill or cook in a skillet until cooked through.
2. In a bowl, combine diced mango, red onion, lime juice, and salt to make the mango salsa.
3. Toast the hamburger bun, then layer with lettuce, the cooked chicken, and mango salsa.
4. Serve immediately.

Peanut Butter and Banana Sandwich

Ingredients:

- 2 slices of bread (whole grain or white)
- 2 tablespoons peanut butter
- 1 banana, sliced
- Honey (optional)

Instructions:

1. Spread peanut butter on one slice of bread.
2. Layer banana slices on top of the peanut butter.
3. Drizzle with honey if desired.
4. Top with the second slice of bread, slice in half, and enjoy.

Sweet and Spicy Pork Bahn Mi

Ingredients:

- 1 baguette
- 1 cup cooked pork, sliced or shredded
- 1/4 cup pickled carrots and daikon radish
- Cucumber slices
- Fresh cilantro
- Jalapeño slices (optional)
- Mayonnaise (or spicy mayo)

Instructions:

1. Cut the baguette in half and spread mayonnaise on both sides.
2. Layer with cooked pork, pickled carrots and daikon, cucumber slices, cilantro, and jalapeño slices if using.
3. Close the sandwich and slice in half to serve.

Crispy Chicken Sandwich with Pickles

Ingredients:

- 1 chicken breast, pounded to an even thickness
- Salt and pepper to taste
- 1/2 cup flour
- 1 egg, beaten
- 1 cup breadcrumbs
- Oil for frying
- 1 hamburger bun
- Dill pickles
- Mayonnaise (optional)

Instructions:

1. Season the chicken breast with salt and pepper. Dredge in flour, dip in beaten egg, and coat with breadcrumbs.
2. Heat oil in a skillet over medium heat and fry the chicken until golden and cooked through, about 5-7 minutes per side.
3. Toast the hamburger bun and layer with crispy chicken, dill pickles, and mayonnaise if desired. Serve warm.

Muffuletta with Olive Salad

Ingredients:

- 1 round loaf of Italian or Sicilian bread
- 1/2 cup olive salad (mixed olives, pickled vegetables, and herbs)
- 6 ounces mortadella, sliced
- 6 ounces salami, sliced
- 6 ounces provolone cheese, sliced
- 2 tablespoons olive oil

Instructions:

1. Slice the loaf of bread in half and drizzle with olive oil.
2. Spread the olive salad generously on the bottom half.
3. Layer with mortadella, salami, and provolone cheese.
4. Top with the other half of the bread, press down slightly, and cut into wedges to serve.

Roasted Beet and Goat Cheese Sandwich

Ingredients:

- 2 slices of whole grain or ciabatta bread
- 1 medium roasted beet, sliced
- 2 ounces goat cheese
- Arugula or spinach
- Balsamic glaze (optional)
- Salt and pepper to taste

Instructions:

1. On one slice of bread, layer roasted beet slices and crumbled goat cheese.
2. Top with arugula or spinach and drizzle with balsamic glaze if desired.
3. Season with salt and pepper, then place the second slice of bread on top.
4. Cut in half and serve.

Enjoy these delicious sandwiches!

Salami and Cheese Sandwich with Mustard

Ingredients:

- 2 slices of Italian bread
- 4 slices of salami
- 2 slices of cheese (provolone or Swiss)
- Mustard (yellow or Dijon)
- Lettuce leaves (optional)

Instructions:

1. Spread mustard on one side of each slice of bread.
2. Layer salami and cheese on one slice.
3. Add lettuce if desired and top with the second slice of bread.
4. Cut in half and serve.

Mushroom and Swiss Burger

Ingredients:

- 1 beef patty (or plant-based)
- 1 cup mushrooms, sliced
- 1 slice Swiss cheese
- 1 hamburger bun
- Salt and pepper to taste
- Olive oil

Instructions:

1. In a skillet, heat olive oil and sauté mushrooms until golden. Season with salt and pepper.
2. Cook the beef patty according to your preference, adding the Swiss cheese on top to melt in the last minute of cooking.
3. Toast the hamburger bun, then layer with the patty, sautéed mushrooms, and any additional toppings (lettuce, tomato, etc.).
4. Serve immediately.

Tzatziki Chicken Wrap

Ingredients:

- 1 grilled chicken breast, sliced
- 1 large tortilla wrap
- 1/4 cup tzatziki sauce
- Lettuce or spinach
- Sliced cucumbers
- Sliced tomatoes

Instructions:

1. Spread tzatziki sauce evenly over the tortilla wrap.
2. Layer with sliced chicken, lettuce, cucumbers, and tomatoes.
3. Roll up the tortilla tightly, slice in half, and serve.

Honey Mustard Ham and Cheese Sandwich

Ingredients:

- 2 slices of bread (whole grain or white)
- 4 slices of ham
- 2 slices of cheese (cheddar or Swiss)
- 1 tablespoon honey mustard
- Lettuce or spinach (optional)

Instructions:

1. Spread honey mustard on one slice of bread.
2. Layer with ham, cheese, and lettuce if using.
3. Top with the second slice of bread and cut in half to serve.

Chickpea and Avocado Smash Sandwich

Ingredients:

- 1/2 cup canned chickpeas, rinsed and mashed
- 1/2 ripe avocado, mashed
- 1 tablespoon lemon juice
- Salt and pepper to taste
- 2 slices of bread (whole grain or sourdough)
- Sliced tomatoes and lettuce (optional)

Instructions:

1. In a bowl, mix mashed chickpeas, avocado, lemon juice, salt, and pepper.
2. Spread the chickpea and avocado mixture on one slice of bread.
3. Add sliced tomatoes and lettuce if desired.
4. Top with the second slice of bread and serve.

Sweet Potato and Black Bean Sandwich

Ingredients:

- 1 medium sweet potato, cooked and mashed
- 1/2 cup canned black beans, rinsed
- 1 tablespoon lime juice
- 2 slices of bread (whole grain or ciabatta)
- Avocado slices (optional)
- Spinach leaves (optional)

Instructions:

1. In a bowl, mix mashed sweet potato, black beans, lime juice, and salt.
2. Spread the mixture on one slice of bread.
3. Top with avocado slices and spinach if desired.
4. Place the second slice of bread on top and serve.

Enjoy these delicious sandwich recipes!

www.ingramcontent.com/pod-product-compliance
Lightning Source LLC
LaVergne TN
LVHW081502060526
838201LV00056BA/2893